the other side
of the door

For all babies who live in the sky.

First published in 2021 by Laura Doyle + Sarah Tobin
First printed and supported by ArrowManagement.ie

ISBN: 978-1-8382387-1-1

Contact us:
theothersideofthedoorjournal.com
Email: theothersideofthedoor19@gmail.com
Instagram: @the_othersideofthedoorjournal

Contents

We're Sorry

We are so sorry for your loss. We've been where you are, and it's devastating.

The purpose of this journal is to act as a comfort blanket. Unfortunately, we can't take your pain away, but we hope that we can offer you some comfort in a time of despair. We hope this journal will help you feel less alone when your world has crumbled. At this moment you might be feeling numb, or be experiencing a sense of shock and disbelief. We know because we are mums who lost our babies too.

This, right now, is most likely, the worst part. But please know you will get through this, even if you never feel the same again.

When we were told there was no hope for our little boy, I remember thinking how would we survive this? The hospital will support you and give you lots of information but what they can't tell you is that you will be ok or this has happened to someone else.

And for me, that's what I craved. I needed to know that someone else had been through this and survived. I remember thinking how would I cope? How would I get through this, how would life go on? I wanted to find other people who had been through this unimaginable loss and know that they were ok.

Laura

The Other Side of the Door

It might not feel like it now, but there is life and possibly hope on the other side of the door. Part of the reason for this journal is to create a safe space for you and your thoughts at this difficult time. It is to share with you stories of loss so that you can know that you are not alone. We hope you can take comfort in any learnings or wisdom these stories impart. Some of them are here in this journal and we are collecting others online (details on the back page).

We have put together thoughts, advice and experience from ourselves and from many others, to aid you on this journey of recovery, wherever that takes you. We have tried to be as inclusive as possible to all situations surrounding baby loss, but not every paragraph will suit your particular situation and apologies in advance for that.

For those of you picking up this journal many moons after your baby has passed on, we hope that you can find comfort in these words despite the benefit of time behind you. Use this journal for whatever you need, to help you at whatever stage you are at.

Life will go on because it has to. You will cope, and you will learn to live with losing your baby. For now, and at any time, it's ok to sit with your pain. Don't be afraid to cry. Please pay attention to how you are feeling and if things are not lifting for you even after using some of the tools included here please seek professional help, perhaps by starting with your GP. You do not have to do this alone, there is so much support out there.

"Love teaches us we can still go on a little more even after falling apart" **- Dhiman**

Sending love,

Laura & Sarah

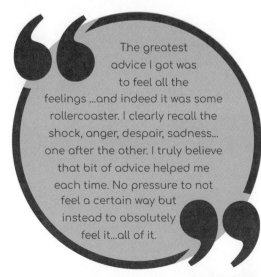

The greatest advice I got was to feel all the feelings ...and indeed it was some rollercoaster. I clearly recall the shock, anger, despair, sadness... one after the other. I truly believe that bit of advice helped me each time. No pressure to not feel a certain way but instead to absolutely feel it...all of it.

Survey Quote

How to use this journal

This journal is for you to use as you need to. We've placed advice on what might come next for you at the front, as well as stories we hope will help, and then we've allocated space for you to write whatever you need.

You might want to write your baby's story. You might use it to take notes at the hospital or plan a funeral or remembrance service. It might be nice to use some of the journal prompts to keep a record of how you feel at this time, something to look back on, some details you will most likely forget. Journaling can be a great tool to allow yourself to start the healing process when you are ready. It can be gentle, mindful and grounding.

Words might escape you right now. You may not even recognise what you feel, you might just feel numb. You might be questioning "why has this happened"' and "what's life all about?" as a result of your loss. Please know that this is normal. You are experiencing trauma and your mind and body are trying to make sense of it all. Writing rather than talking about your experience might be easier. This is your judgement-free space to write what you need to, a place you might come back to again and again in the future.

"I started a blog two months after Alice died. I needed to get words out of my head and found it easiest to type them. Looking back now 6 years later, I am so glad that I've recorded all of the details and the emotions I experienced, as I can't remember them now with the same accuracy. We were also fundraising at the time and I had a place to direct people to learn about our story and Alice's life. I continued to post there for another year or two with follow up stories of our second baby's birth and how I managed that pregnancy." **Sarah**

Journaling tips:

- Keep the pen moving, just let it all out - don't think too much about what you are writing
- Don't worry about spelling and grammar - it is perfectly imperfect just as it is
- When ready, allow yourself to go to the hard and painful places
- Have compassion for yourself, imagine how you would support a friend through this and give yourself that same love and support

Journaling Prompts:
These might be nice to use at some point to start your pen flowing:

- How am I today?
- What's rising in me today?
- Where am I holding pain in my body?
- What emotions am I feeling?
- What could I start to let go?
- What's safe to let go?
- What do I need?
- Who can I ask for help?
- What am I happy for today?
- What am I grateful for in my life right now?

Other ideas:
- Write a letter or regular letters to your baby
- Write a love letter to yourself
- Draw or doodle, colour in
- Use a blank page to write their name in fancy lettering
- Create a scrapbook of photographs, hospital items, poems or cards you received

> "
> I wrote Beau a letter, twice a week on a Tuesday and Friday. Tuesday because it would have marked another week he should have been here. Friday because Beau died on a Friday and it meant another week had passed, in which he wasn't here. Half of what I wrote probably didn't even make sense, but I didn't care! It was never for anyone to read. It was a way of keeping him close and pouring my heart out to him, coupled with all my thoughts and worries. I genuinely found it helped.
>
> **Laura**

WHAT WE'VE LEARNT ABOUT GRIEF

"Grief is just love with no place to go." **Jamie Anderson**

1. Be kind to yourself

We know it's a cliché, but try to put yourself first, you are going through the unimaginable. If you are not ready to talk to or see friends, then don't. They will be ready and waiting when you need them. If it helps, task family and friends with something practical that can help, such as bringing over some home-cooked meals, or taking your dog for a walk, or sprucing up the house before you come home, or getting some food in the fridge. It's often easier to discuss practical tasks at this stage rather than how you are feeling, and that's perfectly ok too.

When you do get some time alone, treat yourself to a nice salt and essential oil bath or a long hot shower, curl up on the couch or go for a walk. Hop into bed or go outside and scream. Prioritise your self-care. We've created a self-care planner at the back of the journal that you can use when ready to plan moments that will start to bring you hope again.

Put one foot in front of the other and do what you can to get you through the day for the moment. You will make it. It may take time, but you will make it.

"I have been kind to myself. Bought nice candles, warm blankets, practiced yoga, gentle meditations, my gratitude journal, I have accepted that my miscarriage was not caused by anything I did." **Survey Quote**

"When you survive loss… everyone is quick to tell you how strong you are, and how tough you must be. But actually, no one has a choice to survive grief, do they… it's not optional. You just have to cry in the shower, sob in your pillow and pray you will make it." **Zoe Clark-Coates**

2. Cry

There is no one size fits all with grief and unfortunately, no one can fix it for you. People can certainly help and if and when you feel ready, talk. Find someone who will listen, be it a friend, family member, counsellor and talk. Don't keep it bottled up. It will only eat away at you from the inside. Acknowledging how you feel is a very important part of the healing process, even if what you are feeling is numb.

Don't be afraid to let it out. I cried daily for weeks. In fact, at one point I wasn't sure I'd be able to stop.

Laura

Let the tears flow and don't put any pressure on yourself. More importantly, give yourself time.

Remember: Crying is good for you. It's self-soothing as it releases oxytocin and endorphins and kick starts the parasympathetic nervous system response, all aiding your recovery. It can also ease physical and emotional pain.

3. Learning from the pain of others

"I realise everyone is different and everyone has their own way of coping but since Beau died, I have found listening to music and podcasts has helped. I made a playlist of songs just for Beau. Initially I couldn't listen to them without crying my eyes out but at the same time I found it a comfort to make something just for Beau and I to share." **Laura**

Here are a few podcasts, blogs and books that have been helpful to so many grieving parents.

Podcasts:

• The Parent Hood – *Marina Fogle*
Episodes:
- 11th Oct 2019 – Supporting parents through baby loss
- 22nd Feb 2019 – Navigating motherhood after loss
- 10th Nov 2018 – In conversation with Elle Wright
- 12th Oct 2018 – Baby loss awareness week
- 10th June 2018 – Miscarriage
- 7th Feb 2018 – Baby Loss: – Navigating life when the plan doesn't go to plan

• The Good Glow – *Georgie Crawford*
Episodes:
- 12th Jan 2020 – Leigh Arnold
- 28th July 2019 – Miriam Hussey

• Everymum The Podcast
Episodes:
- 15th Oct 2019 – Healing from baby loss (Sarah Tobin)
- Season 3 – Sinead Hingston

Blogs:

• featheringtheemptynest.co.uk: Feathering the Empty Nest *by* Elle Wright - this wonderful lady will give you a reason to get out of bed, a reason to keep going and a reason to keep hoping

• onedayofwinter.com: One Day of Winter is about the one day Nicola Gaskin had with her son Winter

- **blogspot.alicerosefrancestobin.com:** Alice Rose's story written *by* Sarah Tobin

- **ourmissingpiece.org:** This site shares many different blogs with real life stories of loss

- **lifelossandlipgloss.com:** Hannah shares her loss of Billy at full term and documents her pregnancy after loss during a pandemic

- **stillmothers.com:** A community for mothers whose only child(ren) have died

- **lossmama.com:** Vanessa shares the loss of her daughter Leah in 2016 having a precious 33 hours with her before she took her last breath

- **uterusmonologues.com:** A blog about life after recurrent miscarriage

Books:

- *Everything* by Zoe Clarke-Coates
- *Saying Goodbye* by Zoe Clarke-Coates
- *Pregnancy After Loss* by Zoe Clarke-Coates
- *Ask Me His Name* by Elle Wright
- *Life After Baby Loss* by Nicola Gaskin
- *The Gifts of imperfection* by Brené Brown
- *When a Baby Dies* by Ronald Nash
- *Loving You From Here* by Susan Clark and Sands
- *The Brink of Being: Talking About Miscarriage* by Julia Bueno
- *Empty Cradle, Broken Heart* by Deborah Davis
- *What I know for Sure* by Oprah Winfrey
- *An Exact Replica of a Figment of my Imagination* by Elizabeth McCracken
- *It's Ok That You're Not Ok* by Megan Devine
- *Life After Stillbirth* by Sarah Nelson (available on Kicks Count UK website)
- *The Uterus Monologues* by Jennie Agg

There are many parents out there sharing their baby loss journey so perhaps connecting with an existing community in time might be something to look into, it can help you feel less alone.

4. Move forward at your own pace

Some parents acknowledge their baby loss both publicly and privately. Some just keep it all private. There is no right or wrong way to grieve the loss of your baby. Do what works for you. Do what keeps you going.

Light a candle daily or only for remembering passing dates. Whatever you do to remember your baby it will be enough.

"In the months following Beau's death, I remember feeling so jealous and sad every time I saw a pregnant woman or new baby. I soon learnt this is normal. I am both happy for those women and babies, but I am so sad and so angry that Beau didn't get to be one of them. I think of all the "firsts" Beau won't get to have and all the little milestones he will miss. I miss him and all that should have been." **Laura**

Don't be hard on yourself. If you find it tough to be around new babies or pregnant friends - that's ok. Give yourself time. After our babies died, we wanted the whole world to stop. We wanted time to stand still. Unfortunately, it doesn't, time ticks on and the world moves with it. But you can *give* yourself time.

Remember: Your baby is always with you. During pregnancy, cells from your baby cross the placenta and enter your body, where they can become part of your blood and tissues.

"Going to a therapist during or after my next pregnancy would have helped my healing journey. I believe if I had gone sooner I wouldn't have suffered such anxiety and burn out this year after my little boy arrived safe and sound." **Survey Quote**

5. Considering pregnancy after loss

I always remember fondly the midwife who helped deliver Beau. As she was leaving, she hugged me and told me she would see me again in different circumstances. At the time I couldn't process what was happening let alone consider getting pregnant again. But in the weeks and months that followed Beau's death, I took comfort in her words. They gave me hope.

Laura

It can be very conflicting experiencing such grief, loss and trauma but also feeling keen to be pregnant again. On one hand, you don't want to dishonour your loss and on the other, you want to feel life is moving forward in a positive direction.

Getting pregnant again can become all consuming, as we try to regain some control of life as we now know it. We know nothing could replace our precious angel babies but the longing to become a mother, or to have a bigger family does not go away.

"As I started to put this journal together, I was so lucky I fell pregnant again a few months later. However, 7 weeks into that pregnancy I started to spot and then to bleed. I miscarried again. There I was back on the other side of the door, in that same hospital, in waiting room B. I often wondered was it referred to room B for the broken women. Was I broken…? For anyone who has experienced the other side of the door, where all hope at that moment is lost, my heart breaks for you." **Laura**

"Good things come to those to believe; better things come to those who are patient, but the best things come to those who don't give up." ***Anonymous***

"I hope the inclusion of my subsequent miscarriage doesn't scare you. The reason I've included it in the journal, is because I learnt something important from it. Mentally I wasn't ready for another baby. I spent so long focusing on trying to get pregnant after Beau died that I didn't even stop to think how I'd feel if I got pregnant again. The truth is I never dealt with Beau's death. I kept it all bottled up, afraid if I spoke my feelings out loud, I would crumble. I spent so long trying to hold it all together that inside I started to fall apart. I would replay the moments of Beau's birth over and over in my mind. When I closed my eyes at night all I could see was his little face and I didn't know how to cope with it. Please don't let this happen to you." **Laura**

After the shock of all this has worn away and you are left with your thoughts, talk to someone. We thought we would manage fine on our own. But in Laura's case it took another miscarriage to literally force her to look at her grief. Find someone, be it a counsellor, a therapist, a friend, a family member, anyone you feel comfortable pouring your heart and your inner fears out to. We've learnt you need support of some kind on this road. Please don't be afraid to ask for help. It's one of the bravest things you can do.

Online support was
a total lifesaver - I found
Joel The Complete
Package (joeltcp.org) and Sands forums
(sands.community) helpful. Leaning on others
who understand more than most helped
no end. Discussing and agreeing a care plan with
maternity services; pushing for better care
and advocating for myself and my baby,
e.g, demanding to see the same consultant
throughout; having more regular community
midwife appointments, more scans, etc; are all
things that helped us so much.

Survey Quote

"Not everything that is faced can be changed, but nothing can be changed until it is faced." **James Baldwin**

On Marina Fogle's *The Parent Hood* podcast, Marina mentioned once hearing a woman say, "grief doesn't go away but you learn to wear the weight of it, and it does get lighter on your shoulders."

It may not seem it now but over time this is very true. It does get easier. Nothing will ever take away the pain of losing your baby. The grief will always be there. But there will come a day when you will be able to say their name aloud without your heart breaking into a million pieces.

I found the gentle birth app very good; I invested a lot of time into doing their meditations and pregnancy affirmations on YouTube were hugely beneficial also for getting me through another pregnancy.

Survey Quote

You will also find happiness again; it may be different to the happiness you previously experienced, but it will come, and you will smile, and you will laugh again. What happened was beyond your control but what you can control is the hope that there will be brighter days ahead. Your loss will always be part of you, your grief will always be valid, but you will learn to live with it and hopefully one day find peace with it.

"I will be like the moon and learn to shine even when I am not whole." **Sabina Laura**

AFTER YOUR BABY HAS DIED

"I struggle to put this into words. I can still remember every moment. We had a little small white blanket at home, which I washed with all our clothes so it would have our family smell. I brought it into the hospital with me for Beau to be wrapped in and the midwife helped dress him in tiny clothes. Take as many photographs of your baby as you want. This is a precious moment to be cherished and remembered. I wish I had taken more of Beau. If I'm honest I was quite frightened to hold Beau after he had passed away. He was so delicate." **Laura**

It can all feel so surreal. The whole situation is so unfair. Why us? Why our babies? We wish we could answer that, both for ourselves and for you. Amid the fog, try to make sure you do all the things you want to do. If you want to kiss and cuddle, bathe and dress your baby, then do.

Take all the memories of these kisses and cuddles. Hold onto them as they will get you through the dark days. You had a baby, he or she will be your child forever and no matter what your love for them will last forever.

Some practical things

After your baby has passed away you may be given a cold cot for him or her. You can usually expect to stay the night in the hospital and perhaps subsequent nights. The hospital will give you a little memory box for your baby, which are very kindly donated. It might take you a while to look at this but in time it is a comfort to have.

The chaplain and bereavement midwives will discuss with you whether you'd like to take your baby home, which we believe can be facilitated by Féileacáin (The Stillbirth and Neonatal Death Association of Ireland – Feileacain.ie) or you may leave your baby in the care of the hospital until you are ready to lay him or her to rest.

We know the pain of losing your baby is unbearable. How are you even supposed to contemplate walking out the door? The feeling of loss and sadness can be utterly overwhelming. Take your time. You will be able to do it. You are so much stronger than you think.

"Hope – if you only carry one thing throughout your entire life, let it be hope. Let it be hope that better things are always ahead. Let it be hope that you can get through even the toughest of times. Let it be hope that you are stronger than any challenge that comes your way. Let it be hope that you are exactly where you are meant to be right now, and that you are on a path to where you are meant to be... Because during these times, hope will be the very thing that carries you through." **Nikki Banas**

"I buried him with a teddy and have the same one with me. Also seeing his name on his headstone is very important." **Survey Quote**

"We planted a weeping willow tree and wrote letters to the baby. We buried them under a tree with a scan picture. Unfortunately we didn't receive our baby's remains back from the hospital." **Survey Quote**

Laying your baby to rest

"We decided to have Beau cremated and had a small prayer service in the Chapel of the Angels – Mount Jerome. I had planned to leave a tiny silver heart inside his little wicker casket with him and I had the other half to keep. However, I only found out on the day of his funeral that you can't add metal objects to the casket when it is being cremated. Thankfully I had also added a comfort blanket for Beau, which I had cut into two, a piece for him and a piece for me. I still sleep with this piece of blanket." **Laura**

Planning a funeral or prayer service for your baby can be very painful. We won't overwhelm you with the logistics and there is usually a chaplain attached to the hospital who will go through this with you. Together, you can plan how you wish to honour your baby. You may decide to contact your local parish priest and local funeral home if you would like to have a funeral service or cremation for your baby. Sadly, many of them will have done this before and will be able to guide you. If you have older children, you may wish to include them in the service. It may act as a way for them to say goodbye to their little brother or sister. Or if you feel they are too young or it is just too painful perhaps you could suggest that your elder child or children draw a picture for their little sibling, which you can lay with your little baby. Do what is right for your family at this time.

"We had Alice cremated in Brighton in a beautiful little chapel. Luckily for us we were able to have over 100 friends and family to celebrate her life. 20 flew over from Ireland, gosh we were so lucky to have such amazing support. We tied colourful balloons to the back of chairs, and my husband Dave wrote the most amazing speech. We played our first dance song which suddenly seemed to fit so perfectly with the day; Les Fleur by 4 Hero.

"We had a small ceremony organised by the hospital and each set of parents were given two small paper hearts – one to place in the grave and one to take home. It sits tucked into the edge of a frame that has a picture of my husband and I in it.

Survey Quote

Driving to the crematorium in the car, I just remember clutching to that white little coffin. That was the hardest part for me, seeing her tiny coffin go behind a curtain. It broke me. I pulled the curtain back for one last look. We included a teddy that Alice had had in her NICU bed and cards we had written for her. Our family also added some in too. We went to a pub afterwards and got to see everyone for the first time since our little hospital bubble. These are very fond memories for us and made us feel so supported and loved." **Sarah**

Music suggestions

It can be overwhelming making all the decisions and in the hope of having to spare you some of the pain of gathering songs, we have listed a few below. Perhaps you have a happy song, one that brings good memories and makes you smile. Again, these are just some suggestions, do what is right for you.

• **Baby Mine** – Bette Midler
• **Somewhere in my memory** – John Williams (Home Alone)
• **Forever Young** – Martin Tallstrom (Acoustic version)
• **Memories** – Maroon 5
• **Somewhere over the Rainbow** – Israel Kamakawiwo'ole
• **Vincent** – Ellie Goulding
• **How long will I love you** – Ellie Goulding
• **All the small Things** – Cloudsmiff (Acoustic version)
• **Little Moon** – MacKenzie Bourg
• **House** – Joshua Moss
• **1,000 Miles** – Mark Schultz (Broken and Beautiful)
• **Tears in Heaven** – Eric Clapton
• **In the arms of an Angel** – Sarah McClachlan
• **The Feather Theme, Forrest Gump** – Alan Silvestri & Jeffrey Michael
• **Follow The Sun** – Xavier Rudd
• **Colours of the Wind** – Caspar Esmann
• **Breathless** – Simply Three (Better Days)
• **Find You** – Canyon City (Constellation)
• **Almost Made It** – Racoon (Look Ahead and See The Distance)
• **Let her go** – Passenger
• **Winter Bear** – Coby Grant

"We had an instrumental version of the song we most associated with her for her actual funeral. This was my husband's idea as it's a quite well known/popular song and he wanted the version from her funeral day to be a bit different. And also, to allow us some space when it did come on the radio to not always go straight back to that day and that room. At the time I couldn't see the point, but it was really good." **Survey Quote**

Registering the death of your baby

Laura found registering Beau's death absolutely incomprehensible, so it took her almost a year to do it. The hospital will give you a Death Notification Form. They will usually have completed Part 1 and you need to complete Part 2. It does state at the top of the form that you need to bring it to any Registrar within 3 months of the death. Laura left it very close to Beau's one year anniversary before she could bring herself to do this and they were very accommodating and kind to her.

You will need to find your local Civil Registration Service, which you can find from the following; https://www2.hse.ie/services/births-deaths-and-mar-riages/contact-a-civil-registration-service.html

Search for your county and the contact information for this office will be there. Usually, you need to attend the office with the form and a copy of your I.D (driver's license, passport recommended) however as we were in the midst of COVID-19 it is possible to do this via email, which may be the case going forward.

We appreciate this is another heart-breaking task, but Laura was so glad she did it.

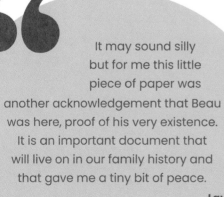

It may sound silly but for me this little piece of paper was another acknowledgement that Beau was here, proof of his very existence. It is an important document that will live on in our family history and that gave me a tiny bit of peace.

Laura

KEEPING MEMORIES ALIVE

It can be very comforting to create traditions, rituals or habits that allow you to remember your baby. These can be used on special days like birthdays, anniversaries, Christmas, or family gatherings - or they can just be things you can do whenever you feel like it.

These traditions might also be a useful way of including immediate or extended family if that feels appropriate for you. Remember there is no right or wrong way to do this, do whatever feels best for you at any given moment.

We've gathered some suggestions and ideas that might inspire your own traditions:

(we are aware not all of these will be applicable, so please take what resonates here)

- Writing messages on stones and throwing them into the sea
- Having a birthday cake to celebrate their birthday each year
- Writing them sealed letters on their birthday to open in the future sometime, maybe an 18th birthday
- Start a fundraiser in their honour for something close to your heart
- Create or fill a memory box for your baby (often these are available in the hospital provided by a charity)
- Find a dedicated space for them like a bench in your favourite park, or a particular spot on the beach where you can go to think of them

- If available transform their ashes into a keepsake or piece of jewellery that you can see or wear often
- If available frame a picture or scan picture where you can see it
- Get the scan picture painted into a beautiful piece of abstract art (quaintbabyart.com)
- Wear jewellery with significance or a date of birth inscribed
- Plant a tree or flower to bloom when baby was due / born
- Create a box frame of teddy, jewellery, baby's wrist band, anything that serves as a memento
- Dedicate or create a Christmas tree decoration for them
- Add your baby's name to the hospital's remembrance book or add it to their Christmas tree
- Have a candle commissioned with their name on it – which you can light on their birthday or anniversary
- Attend or participate in a wave of light ceremony by the hospital, charity or online
- Name your baby
- Talk about your baby to family and friends
- Talk to your baby – out loud or in your head

The hospital made hand and footprints and moulds, friends named a star after Rosie and sent it to us. I also bought crystals to see the beautiful rainbows when the sun shines.

Survey Quote

I have a bracelet with his handprint and name engraved so his hand and mine are always close together.

Survey Quote

We do something as a family the day of her birthday...let off balloons ...the kids draw pictures ...write all our names on the flat stones when we go to the beach

Survey Quote

Talking to your children about their sibling

It can be extremely difficult communicating to your child or children that their sibling is no longer with them. They may not have the comprehension abilities at the time to process this confusing information. It is advised by many psychologists to be very honest and clear.

They will know that something sad has happened as they will sense your moods and see your tears. Please know that this is ok. It is good for them to see you visibly upset and expressing your emotions, this is very healthy. It is important to validate what they are seeing by being honest with what has happened. If they don't get a clear explanation (even if they don't fully understand it), they might wrongly interpret the sadness within you as something they did and internalise it as their fault.

Give them an opportunity to ask questions and talk about the baby even if it is really painful for you at this time. They will likely be able to process the loss quicker and easier if they have this time and honest answers from you. It might even help you on your healing journey also.

Be mindful that they might have changes in moods, could be more clingy, could want to stay away, or want to be very vocal about how they are feeling. All of that is normal too. Be compassionate with yourself and them at this time. It is a lot for a little person to understand.

Here are some books that might help you work through this together:
- *The Invisible String* by Patrice Karst
- **Water Bugs and Dragonflies** by Doris Stickney
- *Always My Twin* by Valerie R. Samuels
- *Perfectly Imperfect Family* by Amie Lands
- *Someone Came Before You* by Pat Schwiebert
- *These Precious Little People* by Frankie Brunker + Gillian Gamble
- *Personalise Your Own Story* at lossbooks.com
- *The Heaven Of Animals* by Nancy Tillman
- *Ivy And The Rock* by Jess Childs
- *Ethan's Butterflies* by Christine Jonas-Simpson
- *We We're Gonna Have A Baby, But We Had An Angel Instead* by Pat Schwiebert

Here are some tips from other parents:

- Include the baby in prayers at night or bring your other children to the grave. Talk and include them.
- Explain to them that their sibling wasn't strong enough to stay on this earth, or that their soul doesn't need a body and stays with us in our thoughts and hearts.
- We just told them we had a baby in Heaven.
- My son is a year old and I bring him out to the tree to say hello and talk to him about our other little baby.
- I always speak about my son to his sister. I will tell her that he wasn't ready to meet me and daddy. She knows he looks after her, and that makes her even more special because she has a very special guardian angel looking down on her.
- Be as honest as possible. Judge each child separately, you will know what they are able for and how well they will process things. Keep them included and allow them to remember their brother/sister.

If you or your child are struggling, consult your paediatrician, general practitioner or a therapist, or reach out to the charities mentioned in the back of this journal.

Our Stories

"One day you will tell your story of how you've overcome what you're going through now, and it will become part of someone else's survival guide."
Anonymous

Thus, the reason for this journal. We hope that by sharing our baby's stories here we can keep their memories alive and offer some hope to you.

That you will be ok. That you will get through this. That you will survive.

Beau Max Doyle

22nd November 2019

I spent eight months of 2019 pregnant. I miscarried at 10 weeks in April. By June and by some miracle I was pregnant again. Cautious and anxious, my husband and I were delighted but hesitant to celebrate. I was now fully aware that not all pregnancies ended with a baby. I had 8, 12- and 16-week scans and check-ups and thankfully all appeared fine. Yet for some reason I felt I just couldn't relax about this pregnancy. At least not until I had the 21-week scan. Our 'big scan' was on the 13th of November 2019 at 11am. If I had a superpower I would go back in time and change that day as some 20 minutes later our world changed forever. There was a problem with our baby's heart. You can be anxious, have your fears and worries but deep down I don't think anyone thinks it could happen to them. The unthinkable just did.

The remainder of the day passed in an absolute blur. We had meetings and scans with the head of foetal assessment, a consultant paediatric cardiologist, a bereavement midwife and a consultant obstetrician & gynaecologist, who had the kindest eyes and an empathy I will never forget. Everything that day was out of our control. The only thing I could find out for certain was the sex of our baby. Our beautiful, longed for little baby was a boy.

In the midst of all the scans we were thrown a lifeline. There was a possibility of travelling to Paris where they may have been able to operate on our baby in utero. It has serious risks, and we would still have one extremely sick baby, but it was a sliver of hope. I don't remember how I walked out of the hospital that day. It was like watching a nightmare unravel while being trapped in it. The following day we got a phone call to confirm our worst fears. Our little baby's heart condition was too serious to consider the operation in Paris. The condition affecting his heart was too severe for him to survive.

I don't think anything, or anyone can prepare you for those words. It's actually hard to breathe. I felt like my heart was going to stop. We were given two options. We could choose to carry our little boy to term. He could pass at any stage and if he did make it to term the chances were, he would not survive the labour. Or we could choose to end the pregnancy. As a parent all you want to do is protect your child. I would have given my little boy my heart if I could.

The reality is there is no choice. There is no right or wrong. In that absolute moment of horror, you have to do what works for you and your partner/family. In our case we had three small children under seven at home. Three little miracles that I am utterly grateful for every single day. After agonising over our heart-breaking options my husband and I decided to end the pregnancy. We did not want our beautiful little boy to suffer. We also had to take into account our other children. For their sake and mine mentally I don't think I could have coped carrying our little boy to term knowing I would never get to take him home.

Nine days later on the 22nd of November my husband and I entered the hospital for me to be induced. We were given a special card so we could just go straight up to the ward and bypass admissions. Almost like a VIP but this is one club no one wants to be in. We were in a single room across from the nurse's station and all I could hear was women in pre-labour coupled with proud partners ecstatically announcing the arrivals of their babies while collecting their partners' belongings. People hovered and chatted outside the room we were in and the hospital went about its business while we waited on the other side of the door. Waiting to deliver a baby who we wouldn't get to take home.

Just after 5:30pm that afternoon I gave birth to our precious little boy. We called him Beau - Max – meaning beautiful and greatest, which he certainly was. He did not cry, and he was so tiny, yet he was absolutely perfect. The midwives placed him on my chest and ten minutes later as quietly as Beau had entered this world, he left it and passed away lying on me, next to my heart. He did not suffer. For those precious minutes we had with Beau all he knew was love because in his short life that is all his Dad and I had to give him. Complete and utter love.

I will always be grateful to the consultants and midwives who helped and supported us and for the compassion we were shown that day. I am also grateful that I could have and hold my baby here in Ireland. In a strange way I consider myself lucky that I unlike thousands of women before me did not have to travel to the UK to end a very much wanted pregnancy.

I wanted to tell Beau's story because I think that sometimes in life there is no right or wrong. Sometimes no matter what you choose the only outcome is pain. I also wanted for Beau to have existed. That he did live in this world and that in his short life all we could give him was unconditional love. My husband and I were blessed to be able to both spend the night with Beau in the hospital. We wept but together we kissed and cuddled him and through our tears we told Beau all about his two big brothers and sister who loved him so much too.

Beau will forever be in our minds and our hearts. He is and always will be part of our family. I will never forget how as he grew; he began to fill my expanding tummy and how his once little flutters turned to kicks. Pure magic, which brought me such sheer joy to feel. I will forever cherish the memory of those kicks. My heart is now the broken one, there will forever be a piece missing but somehow it will be ok because Beau has that missing piece. He will always be with me; he is my first thought in the morning, my last thought at night, he is always only ever one thought away.

"I carry your heart" – ***E E Cummings***

Laura and Dinny Doyle live in County Wicklow with their three children, Jackson, Harvie and Riley. Beau will forever be their fourth baby and while some days are still hard, things have gotten a little easier over time. Together as a family, Beau will live on in their hearts and Laura will do what she can to raise awareness that it's okay to talk about baby loss and miscarriage.

Alice Rose Frances Tobin

20th November 2014

On the 20th of November 2014, I gave birth to our gorgeous girl Alice Rose Frances Tobin. In getting to this point, we had been trying to conceive for a year. I had a wonderful pregnancy and loved every minute of it. I hope Alice felt that love. We are so glad we found out that we were having a girl, as it helped us to have a lovely bond with her even before she was born.

So, the time came to meet our baby. Everything was going well naturally until the last 30 minutes of our 30-hour labour. We don't know quite what went wrong but at some point, during the labour, Alice didn't get enough oxygen. When she eventually was born, by episiotomy, she wasn't able to breathe. The team were quick to respond, and she was immediately transferred upstairs to the Trevor Mann Baby Unit (Brighton). Alice was put on ventilation, and a cooling pad to reduce her temperature for 72 hours to give her a chance of recovery. The lack of oxygen had caused Hypoxic Ischemic Encephalopathy or HIE for short.

At first, I didn't grasp the severity of the situation. I was in shock and thinking positively (like I always try to), and that night I went to sleep thinking I'd be happy to learn sign language in case Alice's brain damage meant she couldn't hear. Dave on the other hand had seen a lot more of Alice's trauma immediately after birth and had understood what the consultant had said about the severity of the situation. I am so grateful to him for letting me grasp the truth at my own pace. About 8 hours after Alice was born, I was wheeled up in my recovery bed (I had to have surgery after the episiotomy) to the 14th floor where I could see her properly for the first time. I will never forget those moments and how responsive she was that first evening.

The consultant talked to us on the second day and went over again how Alice was doing, and how her first night in ICU went. The lack of oxygen had caused her brain to swell with water and was extremely likely that there was irreparable damage. Poor Alice was having regular seizures too, we could see it on the trace (she had plugs in her head to get these readings). The gravity of the situation hit home, and we realised quite quickly that we would have to let Alice go. This was the Friday, and my mum and sister arrived just after the consultant left having flown over from Dublin at 8 am. It was great to have our close family with us throughout. It was agreed that we would wait until the following Monday to have a final MRI scan to confirm the damage and see whether the cooling had helped. This meant we had a few lovely days with Alice before any decisions had to be made.

During those days we sat with Alice, we couldn't hold her until after the 72 hours, but we relished the opportunity when we could. It was difficult as she was hooked up to so many monitors and had many tubes in. We dressed her and washed her with cotton wool and water, I even got to put some expressed colostrum into her mouth on a cotton bud. Our family were able to spend time with her too. We all took turns as it was exhausting being with her all day. We were so lucky to have our close family with us in this bubble for the 5 days, but they were not allowed to touch or hold her, which was sad too.

Day five was the hardest day. We were waiting for the MRI results from a consultant in London, so that morning we spent as much time with Alice as we could. We replaced her white bonnet with a lovely pink one that was sent to us from my mum's friend. She looked so beautiful in it - pink was definitely her colour. We washed her hair and noticed that it was slightly blond - possibly even 'strawberry blonde'! Every discovery and moment with her were a gift, a gift some aren't lucky enough to enjoy. We will treasure everything she gave us.

At 2pm the results came back, and we had a chat with our consultant. The extent of the damage was as we feared, the part of the brain that controls breathing was not functioning, and there was no way she would be able to breathe unassisted. We had to make the difficult decision to take her off life support. We knew this was coming. We had prepared for it. We told all of our family who was with us, and they got some time with Alice to say goodbye.

Alice, Dave, her nurse and I all went into a private family room with a double bed. The nurse took Alice's ventilator tube out of her mouth and we got to see her face without any medical equipment for the first time. She was beautiful, and there was not a mark on her perfect little cheeks. We had three and a half hours with her before she passed. We talked to her, told her how much we loved her, thanked her for choosing us as parents. We told her it was time to go home, to 'fly little bird'. It was her nurse who called her a 'bird' and it really stuck with us. We call her 'Ali-bird' now. We called in all the angels, family and friends who have gone before us to come and welcome her home.

Eventually, she let go. We were so proud of her at that moment but equally devastated. The bubble we lived in had burst, and the reality of what we'd been through hit home. We left the hospital the next day with an empty car seat and no baby girl to settle into a crib that night. That was hard.

We decided to have a celebration of life for Alice. We added 60 colourful balloons to the crematorium chapel to bring a bit of brightness to the day. Over 100 people attended, and the chapel was completely full. We had family and friends fly from Ireland and friends drive long distances in the UK to be there. The Priest (Father Foley from West Cork), who had Christened and Confirmed Alice on day two, cried at the end of the ceremony. He was touched by the number of people there and the amount of love in the room. And he was right, we did feel thoroughly loved and have been completely overwhelmed by the support, messages, gifts, cards and donations that have poured in from all over the world for us and Alice.

Even now we continue to get love and support for our loss, and it has been an instrumental part of our healing process and is so appreciated.

Sarah & David Tobin live in Shoreham by Sea, originally from Dublin, with her two sons Casper and Joshua Tobin, born after Alice. Sarah has healed after the loss of Alice and helps other mums do the same.

Lylah Andi Flynn

6th November 2018

In August 2018 I was pregnant, and my 12-week scan was booked for the 25th of September. It was a day that I will never forget, for all the wrong reasons. It was the day that fundamentally changed our lives forever.

I remember the feeling walking up the steps of the hospital and passing parents with new-born's thinking, that's going to be us again. I couldn't wait. During our scan we heard the strongest little heartbeat, I welled up, I was overwhelmed. The sonographer checked the trans-nuchal fluid on the back of the baby's neck. She looked at the imaging and then my stomach sank. She told us that there was an increased amount of fluid on the baby's neck, just slightly over the normal range, but she thought we should get it checked out. I had a gut feeling that something was wrong. We were sent for Harmony Testing, which checks for chromosomal disorders. The results would take a week to come back. How was I going to go home and function normally, mind the kids, go to work with all this going on?

On Tuesday the 2nd of October, my phone rang, my Harmony Test results had come back with a high probability of Trisomy 18, or Edward's syndrome. I broke down, I couldn't speak, I couldn't think. I curled up on the couch and I cried, the pain was just indescribable, I felt like my heart was literally breaking. Up to that day I had never heard the words Trisomy 18 or Edwards syndrome which is a chromosomal disorder that affects about 1 in 5,000 births in Ireland. It is a Fatal Foetal Abnormality (FFA), because babies with T18 are incompatible with life. I couldn't get my head around it, there was so much information, too much information. I couldn't cope with it, and so I didn't and instead I attempted to convince myself that the blood tests were incorrect, and this was all a big misunderstanding.

The following day, after the Harmony results, we were called into Holles Street Hospital. It was nothing short of horrific. We walked through the main doors of the hospital and into the waiting room where we were surrounded by heavily pregnant women. The consultant was extremely black and white, he said that because of the increased trans-nuchal fluid on our baby's neck, coupled with the high-risk results from the Harmony test he was 90% sure that our baby had Edwards syndrome. The only way to confirm 100% would be to have an amniocentesis, which could not be done until 15 weeks. He continued to talk, I could hear him, but I wasn't really listening, I was literally convincing myself that there was still a chance that he was wrong.

Sadly, the amniocentesis results came back with a confirmed diagnosis of Full T18 / Edwards Syndrome. Our world came crashing down around us and suddenly as a couple we were faced with having to make one of the most awful decisions in our entire time together. The only good thing that we took away from that day was the knowledge that our little baby was a girl. Our little girl and little sister to our three children.

It was October 2018, Ireland had voted back in May on the abortion referendum so we thought if we made the decision to induce the birth early, we would be looked after at home, coupled with the love and support of family and friends. However, we were dealt another enormous blow, because the legislation had yet to be put in place, and if we decided to induce labour we would have to travel to UK.

For us as a couple, there was really no choice. No matter what way we turned, our little girl was not going to stay with us, she was going to die. As much as I would have loved to go full term with Lylah, there were no guarantees, her little heart could stop pre-term, she might not survive the labour and if she did, would she be in pain? Would she suffer for the few minutes or hours she might survive for? Would it be selfish of us to go full term to fulfil our own desires, to hold, kiss and cherish her for a few minutes knowing that it wouldn't be the best decision for her if she were to feel discomfort or pain during that time? We went backwards and forwards trying to decide. In my heart of hearts, I felt that mentally I would struggle to handle another 20 weeks of pregnancy, waiting, wondering, being congratulated on the obvious baby bump that wouldn't have a happy ending. I couldn't stand the thought of allowing myself to get more and more attached to Lylah, knowing that there was an inevitable goodbye at the end – in the end we both decided that it hurts to let go, but sometimes it hurts more to hold on.

Broken hearted we organised our journey to the UK, Lylah would be just shy of 20 weeks. I don't know how we managed it, it's still a blur. We just clung to each other while we navigated a journey that neither of us wanted. Before we left my sister gifted us a 3D scan. I cried the whole way through it, Lylah's heartbeat was strong and she looked perfect to me. There were obvious markers of Edwards Syndrome, Lylah was below average size for the gestation, she had issues with the chambers of her heart and classic facial markers common with the syndrome.

Up until then I had moments where I thought, is there any possibility they could be wrong? But leaving the clinic, in a strange way, although still broken hearted, I felt reassured. It was confirmation that Lylah definitely had Edwards Syndrome and that she just wasn't meant for this world. We got images of her little hands and feet and a lovely clear image of her face – they are precious treasures that I now hold dear to my heart.

On arriving home there was a beautiful gift box with a card, "Shannon Angel Sisters – Hand Crafting Angel Gowns with Love". (These ladies are angels themselves; they take donations of old wedding dresses and they make tiny angel gowns for babies who sadly cannot stay with us). The box contained a beautiful white handmade blanket, a tiny white gown only fit for an angel and the tiniest little handmade baby hat. It was such an unexpected and thoughtful gift, as we hadn't given any thought to what we would dress Lylah in when she was born. Underneath the tissue and garments there were two beautifully written letters, from my sister – one for my husband and I and another addressed to Lylah. To this day, I still cannot read these letters with dry eyes. They stay hidden in Lylah's memory box and I take them out on days when I wish to reminisce, or days when I want to cry, or days when I just miss everything that we so cruelly lost.

Monday the 5th of November arrived, and we left for the UK. It was just horrendous. The induction of Lylah's birth was done over two days and on Tuesday 6th of November at 11:03pm Lylah was born. All we could do was cry, the midwife brought Lylah to be cleaned and dressed so we could spend time alone with her. She was dressed and wrapped in a blanket, they had neatly covered her over and explained that we could remove the cover when we were ready. Together, we took a few minutes, we cried, we were both scared, we didn't know what to expect. We had absolutely nothing to be scared of as Lylah was beautiful. She was tiny but perfectly formed, down to her little eyebrows, fingernails and pouty mouth. We held her, we told her we loved her, we took photos with her, and I whispered into her ear that I was "so sorry".

We travelled home on Wednesday. Lylah stayed close to me all that day, she slept beside me that night, I just wasn't ready to let her go. On Thursday, although I am not a particularly religious person, I went to our local church in Greystones. Lylah, having no birth certificate and no death certificate, could not be buried in consecrated grounds. We decided to bury her at home so she would always be close to us, but I needed a priest to see her or to bless her before we said our final goodbye. My husband expected us to be turned away, knowing that the Catholic Church would not agree with the decision we had made.

Sobbing, I went through the whole story with the priest, he listened, he was kind, empathetic, compassionate – a truly beautiful man and priest – he did not turn us away nor did he make any judgement on us. He asked to see Lylah, we said prayers together and he blessed her for us. He is not aware of this, but I think of him all the time. I will never forget what he did for us that day, and how he surprised us with his compassion and lack of judgement.

We buried Lylah at home later that day, we dressed her in her beautiful white gown, and she was wrapped in the softest white blanket. The children drew pictures for her, I included a photograph of our family of five, and my parents gifted her a miraculous medal. Lylah and her few possessions were laid to rest that day, we planted a white rosebush for her, and we said our final goodbyes. I felt as though my heart was being torn out of my chest.

We have now marked the two-year anniversary of Lylah's birth. I can honestly say to anyone going through a similar situation, you can, and you will get this through this, and I promise you it does get easier. Your broken heart will slowly begin to mend and you will learn to live with the loss. There were very dark days for me in the beginning, and even darker nights. I remember speaking to a counsellor shortly after losing Lylah and telling her that sometimes in the dark of night I would feel upset thinking of Lylah buried outside in the cold and dark and I had fleeting thoughts of wanting to bring her back inside. She explained that grief affects us all in different ways but that you have to pass through all the stages of grief to make it out the other side. There is light at the end of the tunnel, you just need to give yourself time to heal.

Remember that you are not alone, there are others who have walked this path or are possibly going through it with you. I felt utterly alone until I joined a Whatsapp group called, "Leanbh Mo Chroí", for women who have gone through a similar journey to me. They saved me, hearing their stories, knowing I wasn't alone and having a safe place to vent or to admit feelings of guilt really helped me through. They knew and understood what I was going through and were there to offer support, a listening ear or advice whenever I needed it. Please do not suffer alone. Seek out others who know and understand what you are going through, their support is worth its weight in gold.

There isn't a day that goes by where I don't think about Lylah, but I can go weeks or months without shedding a tear. Then out of the blue I may hear a piece of music or a white feather may blow across my path and the emotions come flooding back. They are not the bitter tears from the early days, these tears are shed slowly and silently, and they dry up as quickly as they appear. But I am happy that I still shed tears for Lylah because they are a testament to how much I wanted, love and miss her. I let them flow and they help my soul to heal.

I still question whether I make the right choice for Lylah. I will never know for definite; and nobody can answer this question for me. But what I do know was that a little life was growing inside me, she was made out of love, and was so, so wanted. I felt her flutter inside me and my love for her grew each day. No matter what way we turned, whatever choice we made, Lylah was never going to stay with us. She was not meant for this world and so we chose to let her go early, without any suffering or pain and only ever knowing love.

Someone close to me once told me that the strongest thing in the world is "love", but stronger again is a mother's love for her child. Lylah Andi Flynn, I hope and pray every day that I made the right choice for you. Always remember that you hold a piece of my heart in your little hand, and my heart will never be completely whole until we meet again – I love you always and forever xx

Sophie Keenan

2nd of March 2020

Our beautiful little girl Sophie was born on the 2nd of March 2020, twelve weeks and three days premature weighing two pounds and five ounces. After eight weeks in the Rotunda NICU our little angel gained her wings.

When I was nineteen weeks pregnant my waters broke. I didn't even know that was possible that early on in pregnancy. I quickly became aware of the condition Preterm Premature Rupture of Membranes (PPROM) where the sac surrounding the baby ruptures. Once the sac is ruptured the mother has an increased risk of infection as well as an increased chance of going into premature labour.

For eight weeks I was scanned regularly and continuously given a 'poor prognosis' from consultants. The likelihood of our baby's lungs being developed properly was very slim as the crucial weeks for lung development are between nineteen and twenty-three weeks and our baby had a lack of fluid from nineteen weeks. It was an unbelievably stressful time carrying a baby that we didn't know would survive or not and constantly on edge worrying about either developing an infection or going into labour.

To add to the complications, it was suspected that I had Placenta Accreta – a serious pregnancy condition when the placenta grows into the uterine wall so would require a specialised team for delivery and in some cases a hysterectomy. Thankfully after an MRI scan it was confirmed that I didn't in fact have this condition, the worry that I possibly did have this condition took a lot out of me.

Three days after having the MRI I started to bleed. My husband took me straight to hospital and after being closely monitored in the labour ward for two days as well as receiving steroid injections, I developed an infection. I was taken straight to theatre for an emergency section and put under general anaesthetic.

We had found out the day before that we were having a little girl, so we had both agreed on the name Sophie. I will never forget the panic of being woken up after the delivery asking, "Is she ok?".

A paediatric consultant, whom we had met previously, came to inform us that they had been able to ventilate Sophie and she was doing ok. She weighed over a kilo which was a pleasant surprise as all the growth scans we'd had in previous weeks estimated her to be much less. I felt a huge sense of relief that Sophie was here and doing ok, albeit fully aware that we were going to have a long NICU journey ahead of us.

We already had two children, Jessica 5 and Oisín 2. Oisín had been six weeks premature due to Placenta Previa, he spent twelve nights in NICU after being born which was tough at the time but absolutely nothing in comparison to the journey we were about to begin with Sophie.

After the delivery I was taken to the High Dependency Unit as I was very sick from the infection. It was far from the usual high you would expect after having a baby nor was I ecstatic texting my family and friends about our new arrival. My husband could go and visit Sophie a couple of hours after she was born but while he was in the NICU she began to deteriorate, and he was asked to leave. A while later the consultant came to inform us that Sophie was doing better, and they would keep us informed. It wasn't until the next day that I got to go and visit Sophie, I had already been that mum who struggled to get out of bed and into a wheelchair to be taken to the NICU to see her baby in an incubator so it was hard to believe I was in that position again. I couldn't wait to see Sophie, she was so tiny and delicate and covered in tubes, but she was beautiful.

Having a baby in NICU is the most unnatural thing in the world. You feel like you have absolutely no control. The only thing I could do for Sophie was express breastmilk, talk to her and touch her through little doors in her incubator. I used to read her stories and tell her about where we lived and about her big brother and sister. I used to day dream about the day we got to take Sophie home from hospital and I always tried to stay positive for her.

I cannot even put into words how difficult the eight weeks that Sophie spent in NICU were. The country went into lockdown two weeks after Sophie was born, dads were no longer allowed in NICU and there was a period where mums were only allowed in for fifteen minutes. We lived an hour drive from the hospital so between the commute and trying to look after our two children at home as well as my husband trying to work it sort of felt like we were living somebody else's life. I did get regular visits from the Hospital Chaplain and a Psychologist that worked in the hospital so it was great to get this support as the NICU can be a lonely and frightening place.

Sophie's NICU journey involved many lows and traumatic events with the main issue being her lungs. When Sophie was twelve days old, she developed pneumonia and was very unwell, when she was a month old, she was transferred to Crumlin to have a duct closed in her heart. Sophie took a bad turn a few days after the surgery and we got a phone call in the middle of the night to let us know that Sophie was on maximum support and if things didn't improve in the next day then she wasn't going to be in a good place. It was a level of stress like no other. When I went up the next day Sophie had improved so we could relax a little.

The next few weeks was a series of ups and downs and a lot of difficult conversations. When Sophie was seven weeks old I insisted that I wanted to hold her. I held her first when she was ten days old and the day she turned seven weeks I got to hold her for the second time. It was the most alert she had been that day and when I was holding her she was looking straight at me and I felt pure love, I'm sure she felt it too as all the nurses surrounded us and were amazed at how content she looked and all her stats were completely stable. I got to hold her every day for the next three days, the skin to skin contact was magical and I felt that Sophie had turned a corner that week and things were looking good. However, within a few days Sophie began to deteriorate drastically. On Sunday the 26th of April I was told to bring my husband the next day as the consultant needed to speak to us. On Monday the 27th of April we walked into the NICU, there was a screen surrounding Sophie's corner and we heard the dreaded words 'I'm sorry but there's nothing more we can do for Sophie'.

We were given the choice of turning off Sophie's ventilator or waiting for Sophie to pass away herself over the next few days. As it was important for the two of us to be with Sophie when she died, we decided to turn off the ventilator. I asked the consultant how long it would take for Sophie to die after they switched off the machine and she explained that it usually takes half an hour to an hour but because Sophie's lungs were so bad then probably less. It took Sophie over two hours to pass, I held her in my chest and my husband stroked her head, we sang to her and told her we would love her forever and told her to go to sleep. This ordeal will traumatise us for the rest of our lives, a living nightmare that no parents should ever have to go through. Nothing could have prepared us for this, but we did have the incredible support of the hospital staff to help us through that day.

The hospital Chaplain was our rock that day, she baptised Sophie for us the morning she died, she organised the coffin and she sat with us the whole time Sophie was dying. The NICU staff were also so supportive and we will be forever grateful for the compassions they showed us, particularly on that day. It takes a special type of person to work in a NICU and I don't know how they do their job. A few weeks later when we were back in the hospital one of the nurse managers pulled me aside and said I know you think this is just a job and we move on from one baby to the next but we never forget these babies and we will never forget Sophie. I found this hugely comforting.

After Sophie died, I gave her her first and last bath and got her dressed into a little white knitted dress. She was taken to the Little Chapel in the hospital. The next day the staff came to pay their respects and described Sophie as a 'remarkable little lady' and a 'very special baby'. They did a guard of honour for us leaving the hospital which was such a kind gesture. Leaving a maternity hospital with your baby in a coffin was beyond heart breaking. It's just so wrong. We had a small ceremony for Sophie with our family and close friends and she is buried close to our home.

The days and weeks after Sophie died were incredibly difficult. The only people I wanted to see were my family and close friends. I couldn't hold it together at all, my heart was absolutely broken. People used to say to me 'one day at a time', 'just focus on putting one foot in front of the other' and 'be kind to yourself'. So that's what I did. I joined some groups on Facebook with A Little Lifetime and Feileacain and I did find it comforting to read other people's stories as it made me feel less alone, after all unless you've lost a child yourself you will never understand the true pain of it.

Trying to explain death to a five-year-old and a two-year-old was and continues to be a challenge. We got advice from the Chaplain on how to explain it to the children and she told us to really exaggerate how sick Sophie was because if we just say she got sick and went to heaven then it may cause them to panic if somebody close to them gets sick. We still get random questions thrown at us about death and heaven so we just try to be as honest as we can and keep it was simple as we can. Sophie is very much part of our family, we have memories of her all around our home, we are not afraid to talk about her and whenever someone I don't know asks me about my children I tell them about Jessica, Oisín and Sophie.

My advice to any parent who is faced with the absolute heartache of losing a baby is to reach out and seek as much help as you can as you will struggle to do it alone. As difficult as it is, talking about your baby and your experience helps you to heal.

Grace Murray

16th September 2019

I was 11 weeks and four days pregnant when I began to bleed. I was on duty as a Nurse and I hadn't told any of my colleagues I was pregnant yet. I emerged from the toilet and went straight to the manager. In the office hot tears stung my face as I tried to tell her I was pregnant and bleeding. Short sharp breaths were all that came, I was starting to panic. Eventually I caught my breath and could speak again explaining to my manager what had happened. I rang Paul to come and collect me early. Thankfully my parents were minding our two children and he was already home from work. We went straight to the maternity hospital where I was due to have a booking appointment exactly a week later. I went to A&E and gave a urine sample as requested. I had stopped bleeding. I had no idea what was going on. About an hour ago it looked like I had started my period and now nothing. "What are you doing here?" I thought to myself instantly feeling silly and like I had caused a big fuss over nothing. I had no pain, no cramps, no symptoms at all, this was so confusing. I was triaged and told to come straight into the examination room if I had any gushes of blood or further bleeding. "Did she think I was miscarrying?" I wondered. I had no idea what to think.

I was called into the examination room with the doctor and midwife on duty for the night shift. I really felt like I was wasting people's time having come here as I had stopped bleeding at this stage. I was checked over and everything was fine until my bloated tummy was scanned. Myself and my husband had decided not to have an early scan as this was our third child. We had planned this baby so knew our dates and we had the patience this time to wait for our booking appointment for a scan! I was filled with excitement at the thoughts of our first glimpse of our little baby.

However more confusion followed, as the baby on the screen didn't measure up to a 11 weeks and four days baby, it only measured up to eight weeks and two days. "Maybe your dates are wrong?" the doctor suggested. Not possible for us to be out by three weeks, that was like a month, a cycle, no way was I out by three weeks. And why was there no movement on screen, no flicker of those 2 little hummingbird heart valves flapping away? I was perplexed. The doctor explained that at this early stage of pregnancy

an internal scan would be best for viewing the baby and I was given
an appointment for the Early Pregnancy Unit. I wasn't eight weeks pregnant
though. "I'll check my dates again when we get home, maybe I did count
them wrong", I remember saying to Paul. We went home and my parents
stayed the night with us as it was late when we got back.

I couldn't sleep that night. I checked and rechecked my dates and just
couldn't figure out how I'd be out by three weeks! My head was in a spin,
I was beating myself up saying I overreacted to the bleed and I was being
dramatic. All would be fine, and I'd go to the Early Pregnancy Unit, like
the doctor said, maybe my dates WERE wrong. All I could see when I closed
my eyes was our little baby that didn't move or have a flickering
hummingbird heartbeat visible on what must be outdated equipment.
That morning I had spotting and my heart sank. I had been over the dates
a thousand times and I was not out by three weeks.

I had no idea what to do, how do you wait around a whole week for this next
appointment? Paul booked us in for a scan privately for a second opinion.
The sonographer confirmed our worst fears, there was no heartbeat
present. It wasn't just the old equipment in the hospital. Our baby was dead.
My chest felt like an elephant had moved into it and those hot burning tears
streamed down my face again. I left and made Paul go back for the pictures.
They weren't given to us. How had I just had a baby scan and come out
without scan pictures to look lovingly at the whole way home in the car
contemplating which one to send onto our families. This felt like a nightmare.
So many questions flooded my mind, was this a miscarriage? If my baby
was dead, why didn't I know? Why wasn't I still bleeding? Why was there
no pain? Another week for this appointment, what do I do now? Do I go back
to work? I was in a daze. I rang my best friend who is also a nurse and told
her what was happening. She advised me to ring the hospital again
and bring the appointment forward. I was so exhausted when I got home.
My parents were shocked and stunned that our little baby had no heartbeat.
I had to send my family a text as I just couldn't speak. Paul's parents were
away, we couldn't ruin their holiday with this news.

My appointment was brought forward and the next day I was back
in the maternity hospital in the EPU and an internal scan was performed.
The doctor and midwife confirmed there was no heartbeat, and this was
a miscarriage. It was handled very compassionately, and Paul and I were
given a moment with our scan picture which was offered to us. The doctor

then gave me three options, let nature take its course, take tablets to induce miscarriage or to have surgery. Having two children to think about we agreed the tablets would be the most convenient option and we went home to our house. We sent my parents home and I called into my good friend to tell her what was happening. Sadly, she had experienced her own miscarriage and was able to brief me on what it would be like. I had searched but it was too upsetting for me. The doctor had suggested that we wait until tomorrow to take the tablets as I would have an uncomfortable night, but Paul pointed out that if we waited until morning and we needed to go to hospital the traffic would be an issue. His intuition was right. I took the tablets that evening and a few hours later I began cramping and passing gushes of blood with huge clots again and again and again. We had been informed that this may happen, so we rang A&E and they told us to come in straight away.

My sister was over to mind the children who were asleep, and Paul took me to the hospital. I sobbed as I sat on a black bag and two folded beach towels. The road we were speeding up is notorious for speed checks, so Paul rang the Gardai to tell them he was rushing his wife to hospital as she was having a miscarriage. I started to tell Paul that if I became unresponsive that I'd have just fainted and get me straight to the hospital. Don't stop, just keep going. This was like an out of body experience. When we got to the maternity hospital and parked, I bawled crying.

I was petrified, afraid to move in case another big gush of blood came. This was it; we were losing our baby and it was horrific. Paul got a wheelchair and he bolted into A&E with me where I was expected. My vital signs were checked, an IV line inserted, fluids flew in and my bloods were taken. I was examined and it was then discovered that my pregnancy sac was stuck in my cervix. I was told to push down into my bottom while the Doctor removed our pregnancy sac with forceps. We delivered our baby. What happened next caught me completely off guard.

A form was handed to me to decide where our foetal tissue would go, back to us for our own arrangements or into the hospital plot. Paul was texting my sister to let her know I was ok and check in on the kids, I was so relieved it was all over, and I had survived. The doctor was waiting for me to sign the form, so that meant my baby was in a specimen pot going to the lab, Oh God. More bewilderment, I signed the form as I thought to myself "funerals are for stillbirth and pregnancies that are further along, don't be silly, the hospital plot will do". I signed the form and away they went. My teeth started to chatter, and I shook from head to toe as I was reassured that it was just my body filling with adrenaline after losing so much blood. It is also what happened to me after delivering my other two babies. I stayed the night in hospital and had a dilation and curettage the following day as an internal scan revealed I still had a lot of clot in my womb. It was Friday morning and I was asked going into the theatre how many weeks was I? 12 weeks today, but I wasn't, was I? I certainly wouldn't be 12 weeks when I woke up from surgery.

The grief that followed was like no other, I felt like a part of me was gone, the light inside me was dull and all that kept me going was knowing I had my two children. They were my light, my hope, my tonic on the days where I was filled with longing, despair, loss and disbelief. Family and friends rallied around me to get me back on my feet and in two weeks I was back doing the school run again like nothing had ever happened. I felt so disconnected from myself. About three weeks after the miscarriage I got my period again. A stark reminder every month for the following six months of what I had lost, what "wasn't meant to be" as people told me. The children would ask me why I was crying, I would tell them I missed the baby that was in my tummy but was now in heaven. Our due date came which is my Nanny's Anniversary and we decided to have cake and named, our little angel Grace. Naming her was so important for me, her little life as short as it was, provided us with such excitement and love for her.

She was a part of our family and I don't want her to be remembered as "my miscarriage" or "the baby that died in Mammy's tummy". Time is the best healer for grief and there is no correct way to grieve. It hits us all in waves and when you least expect it! Have compassion for yourselves at this terribly difficult time. A loss is a loss no matter what stage of pregnancy you are in. A positive pregnancy test is life changing! I really struggled with validating my own grief and found people's reactions to baby loss so awkward. This made me question my grief like I should just be getting on with things as it wasn't meant to be. I got a frame from my sister to put my scan picture in and it was such a comfort to me. Having Grace has been life changing like any other new addition, it's just the outcome wasn't what we expected. Be gentle with yourself in this vulnerable time and try to take each day with Grace and ease.

Hugo Jack Ingles

24th April 2019

I am a midwife, originally from Spain, and a mother of three beautiful and special children. Carla, six years old, Claudia Joy, four months old and our little baby Hugo Jack. He was born on the 24th April 2019 with a birth defect called congenital diaphragmatic hernia (CDH), where the diaphragm failed to fully form allowing the abdominal organs to move to the chest cavity, pushing the heart and not letting the lungs grow. We gave him every chance, and enjoyed every minute of his pregnancy knowing that it might be the only few memories that we might have. He was born in the National Maternity Hospital, and was looked after by an incredible team of professionals that went above and beyond to save him, but unfortunately, he couldn't survive. His lungs were just too underdeveloped. He died in my arms surrounded by his family and friends and we were given memories to treasure for life.

Hugo, in four hours and 24 minutes, touched many hearts, and ever since that day we have received nothing but love, gifts and lots of magic from him. To mention the most incredible one, I was able to donate nine litres of breastmilk in Hugo's memory. For me it was such a natural thing to do, and I was supported by my husband, family and friends. Being able to see that liquid gold going to all those premature babies that needed it, gave sense to the senseless situation of being postpartum, with empty arms, sore stitches, and full breasts leaking milk that had no place to go. I felt that my body was crying for him too.

I would like to thank the National Maternity Hospital, with special mention to Dr McParland, Cecilia Mulcahy, Dr Walsh, Dr Curley, Dr Vavasseur, Donna, Lorraine, Rachel, Ann, Val, Dr McCarthy and the bereavement team in Holles street and Helen, the chaplain, for their kindness and compassion throughout the hardest experience of my life. Also, special mention to Féileacáin, because without their support we would not be as well as we are. It is a charity that deserves to be supported, as they do so much for all the families that go through baby loss.

CDH Ireland and UK, were and are an incredible support and a place to find friendships that are gifts, and there is so much comfort in meeting all the little heroes that survived this terrible birth defect.

During the pandemic, I found myself in a difficult situation, not being able, from a mental health point of view, to work and help my colleagues in these unprecedented times. Also, I am from Spain, so I was also dealing with the fear of watching the news and the effect of the Covid-19 in my country, always aware of the possibility of being not being; able to travel home if needed.

I had Carla, our daughter to think about too, who has also had a very difficult year trying to understand why Hugo is not on earth with us. The pressure and emotions that I felt were even more evident and intense as we approached Hugo's first birthday and anniversary - the 24th of April. We had many plans for the day but all had to be cancelled and a very intimate party was organised at home. We didn't feel a bit lonely as the post box filled with cards, and the phone did not stop ringing... flowers arrived and filled the house with a fresh smell. Balloons, cakes and nice messages filled my heart with love. It was a day that I dreaded, and that I thought I would be devastated, but our little Hugo once again spread his magic, and on his birthday, we found out that a new little miracle was joining our family. Carla and Hugo's little rainbow baby sister was on her way for Christmas. We were over the moon, as our much-desired baby was growing in the womb. And even though more than ever the huge gap that Hugo left in my chest was evident, we were starting to see a bit of a bright light coming our way.

We will always remember this lockdown as the time where we got even more time together as a family, and when Carla's biggest dream of having a baby came true. We played, we laughed and we healed a bit more. We saw us becoming a family of 5 in about 2 weeks. I also published our book "Tears and smiles for Hugo" ("Lágrimas y sonrisas por Hugo"), as I found it really hard to see the reaction in Spain towards baby loss. A lot of people did not want to meet Hugo, or talk about his story, so I felt he pushed me to do it, again his magic... to try to change the world a little bit. For now, our hope is that the Spanish piece will be translated into English soon.

I'd also like to take this opportunity to thank all the people who have shown us what friendship and pure love is. We have been so supported and minded since our son's diagnosis that we are forever grateful.
To our families and friends - THANKS

Bodhi Stoney

22th September 2020

My baby was ten weeks old when he died inside my uterus. I found this out alone, with a midwife, mid-scan.

One in four women miscarry. This is a sad statistic of which so many women are unaware. I knew it was a possibility, but I didn't know that my heart would also break. I did not know that the grief would surround me in waves. My loss didn't feel like some version of a period. It felt like some version of a death.

I became pregnant very quickly, just like the first time. I have a 23-month-old boy. His birth was traumatic. It took me a long time to come to terms with that, but my pregnancy with him was without fault.

When I found out I was pregnant for the second time, my mind immediately went to birth. As women we know not to think forward like that. But my first pregnancy had lulled me into a false sense of security. It was the birth that I was worried about, not the pregnancy.

By week ten, I was cautiously having conversations with my baby when we were alone together. I had a name for him. He was our tiny, beautiful secret. I cradled my tummy in our bed, and silently told him 'night night'.

What follows is graphic. Because what happened to me was graphic. I am telling this story because I wish I had read it. The shock would have been less for me, had I known what was coming. Women suffer so much in silence.

The bleeding started on Wednesday. It was light. I rang Holles Street and they reassured me, bleeding during the first trimester is very normal. The bleeding continued over the course of a few days. By the following Monday, despite being consistently calmed and told that everything was fine, I felt deep down, that something was off. I went to Holles Street alone on my lunch break.

I was brought to a room as the midwife gently and kindly scolded me. I was reminded again that light bleeding was normal in the first trimester. In conspiratorial tones, she said, "Won't it be nice to get a sneak peek at your baby now?" I felt safe. I felt relieved. I had been silly.

She performed an ultrasound and turned the screen to show me my perfect little child. There he was. The second time seeing a human inside you is no less astonishing. We both smiled. The image wasn't clear, so she was going to perform a transvaginal scan. With the bleeding, this was not a comfortable experience, but I didn't mind.

Time passed. A few minutes or maybe seconds into the scan, I looked to her face. Reassurance didn't come. She turned the screen away. She frowned and dug deeper into me, moving her device from left to right and tilting her head from side to side. The feeling in the room changed. Those words that you never want to hear. "I am just having a little difficulty finding the heartbeat..."

The next bit feels blurry. I did not cry. I expected her to find it. I told her to look for as long as she needed. There must have been a mistake. I had been silly. She stopped. She went to get a doctor. The doctor checked my cervix. The tears came. I took off my mask and used it to wipe the mascara from my face.

The baby was measuring small, and they still couldn't find the heartbeat. The midwife sat on the bed, went to put her hand on my leg, and then remembered the world we now live in, and took it back. She told me, "I have to be honest. The prognosis is not great here. But we can't be sure; you need to come back in a week." I had to come back in a week for another scan. They needed to measure the baby again to see if it had grown. That was how they would tell if it was alive.

I left the hospital and went to my car and shook. I watched a man get out of the car next to me with an empty baby car seat, grinning ear to ear. I felt like a sad woman in a story. I rang my husband. I couldn't explain what had just happened. I sat in that car for a long time.

The following week I bled more and more heavily. I felt weak and like I was having a painful period. I had no energy. Clots started to pass. I continued to work and minded my son from bed. I told very few people what was happening. I rang my mum and sobbed.

And then one morning, as my son and husband ate breakfast downstairs, I passed my second child. I caught him, fully formed and still in the amniotic sack, before he fell into the toilet. I don't know what noises came out of me in the following moments. I crawled out of that room. I wailed and wretched.

Downstairs my son ran to the stair gate, scared at the noises coming from upstairs. I dried my eyes, put my second child into a jewellery box, and went downstairs to hold my first.

I know how difficult it is to read these words. It is difficult to write them. I do not want sympathy or to indulge in my sadness. Miscarrying is devastating. More devastating than I ever could have imagined. I want people to know that this is happening to women, women you know, all the time.

In the last two weeks, I have been fine, and I have been not fine. So, I have talked. Talking has helped. For me, sharing the bad is as important as sharing the good. I did not want to shoulder this loss alone. I wanted my friends and family to grieve with us. I rang my granny. I rang my closest friends. I rang the Miscarriage Association of Ireland helpline. Women rallied around me and they lessened our pain.

I wanted people to understand, and to know what to say. But so many people don't. It makes them uncomfortable, because it's awful, and they are so rarely confronted with it. So let me tell you, all you need to say is "I am sorry". We don't need to hear that we are lucky because we already have a child, or that it happens to so many women, or that it is nature's way. I know those words come from a loving place, but they don't help the pain.

We need to share our stories and our pain. No loss is the same. No loss is comparable. But sharing will mean feeling less alone. No mother should feel isolated in these moments.

We buried our baby in a jewellery box with a letter that I wrote to him. His brother sprinkled Mayo sand below him and we planted snowdrops above him. My mum and dad stood nearby. On a rainy October day, we said goodbye and we will always remember.

A friend described him as a star in the sky, who will always look down and watch over our little family. Night, night, little one.

More Stories

After losing her son at 19 weeks' gestation, journalist and editor Yvonne Hogan set up a dedicated section on **independent.ie/babyloss** where women and men have shared their stories of miscarriage, stillbirth and neonatal death. The section serves as a testament to the women and men who share their stories, a memorial for the babies lost and as a resource for other people who have gone through or are going through the experience.

Your Story

Your Baby's Name: _____

Date: _____

Hope is the thing with feathers, that perches in the soul and sings the tune without the words and never stops at all.

Emily Dickinson

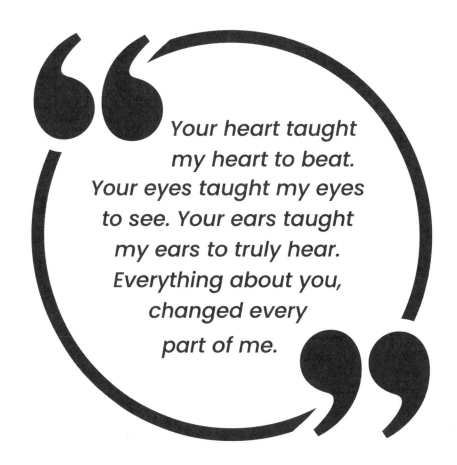

Your heart taught my heart to beat. Your eyes taught my eyes to see. Your ears taught my ears to truly hear. Everything about you, changed every part of me.

Zoe Clark-Coates

When you can't look on the brightside, I will sit with you in the dark.

Peaceful Warrior

I love you with neither my heart nor with my mind. My heart might stop. My mind might forget. I love you with my soul, because my soul never stops or forgets.

Rumi

MY SELF-CARE PLANNER

How to use the planner

Many of us are on the cusp of physical, emotional and mental burn out. Some of us have already been there. And yet we keep going. We keep giving to those around us, and especially in times of shock and trauma we can neglect ourselves.

This planner is to be used to check in with yourself, to remind yourself of all of the things that light you up, and bring you joy, as well as rest and nourishment for the mind, body and soul. Then you can use the planner to schedule these things into your day, week and month.

Use this planner to identify where you need help in order to allow you to do your activities. You can use it to help communicate your needs to your family and even use it as a family plan so everyone has an opportunity to schedule in something just for them.

Come back to this plan as often as you need, and if you go off track, get a new planner out and start again. Use it to connect with yourself regularly to check that you are looking after your mind, body and soul; without one side the pyramid falls apart.

Red Flags & Non-Negotiables

Red Flags are signs that we are not living life in a harmonious way. These could be low tolerance, irritability, lack of patience, tiredness, feeling unsupported, being unwell or sick, feeling emotional...

Identify what those red flags are and list them in your planner. They are telling you there is an imbalance, so that's the time to revisit the plan, and schedule in more activities, rest and joy.

Non-negotiables are the items on your list that bring you the most nourishment and or joy. Have a few of these circled in your planner as priorities for your day, week or month.

When life takes over and you become very busy and start to feel overwhelmed, that is the time to schedule more of these particularly important activities.

This Self-Care Planner is brought to you by **Sarah Tobin**, Creator of Tapping for Mums and the **'Tapping into...with Sarah Tobin' Podcast. tappingformums.com** or IG **@sarah_tobin**

MY SELF-CARE PLANNER

What lights me up?

My Red Flags

Daily

Mind

Body

Soul

Date: _____

Weekly	Monthly

NON-NEGOTIABLES: circle 1 item per square, schedule into your diary, tell your family, schedule as much as you can and schedule more things when you are particularly busy. **TIP:** Tick things off as you achieve them!

CHARITIES

We are honoured to share the details of three separate Irish Charities that might be able to support you and your family at this time.

A Little Lifetime Foundation

We'd like to firstly acknowledge the selfless work of Laura and Sarah, who, having experienced the heart-breaking trauma of losing their babies, then sought to support others through the creation of this beneficial journal.

A Little Lifetime Foundation was established by a group of bereaved parents back in 1983. Today we are a national charity supporting parents whose baby has died around the time of birth or shortly afterwards, and parents who receive a diagnosis of fatal foetal abnormality in pregnancy.

We provide a wide range of free support services to bereaved parents, including parent support meetings, one-to-one counselling, creative workshops, Facebook groups and Remembrance Services. We hold regular newly bereaved meetings which take place over 4 weeks and are hosted by a professional bereavement therapist. These are specifically for parents whose baby has died within the last 12 months. At these meetings we hope you'll find great understanding and support from this shared experience with others also starting out on this sad journey.

We're here to support you and help you through those darkest days, so get in touch.

alittlelifetime.ie
Tel: 01 8829030   **Email:** info@alittlelifetime.ie
Charity Number: CHY11507

Pregnancy and Infant Loss Ireland

This website is a directory of support services and knowledge for parents bereaved through pregnancy loss and perinatal death and at healthcare professionals who care for parents and families bereaved through pregnancy loss. It does this by signposting parents to support and professional services. It directs healthcare professionals to professional supports, clinical care pathways and education programmes.

pregnancyandinfantlossireland.ie

Féileacáin

Féileacáin (Stillbirth and Neonatal Death Association of Ireland – SANDAI) was formed in 2009 and subsequently registered as a charity in 2010. Féileacáin was formed by a group of bereaved parents to offer support to anyone affected by the death of a baby around the time of birth, and the organisation is now the national charity supporting families affected by perinatal loss.

Féileacáin is a volunteer led organisation and receives no funding from the central government, relying instead on the support of communities and the families who avail of their services.

These services, some of which include providing parents with memory boxes, remembrance candles, cuddle cots, sibling support, clothes for babies who are born too little as well as vital advice and support – are all provided free of charge to the hospitals and their delivery is supported by a nationwide team of Féileacáin volunteers. These services are an invaluable comfort and can be a lifeline for bereaved parents.

feileacain.ie
Tel: Support line 085 2496464   **Tel:** Office 028 51301
Email: admin@feileacain.ie
Charity Number: CHY19635

The Miscarriage Association of Ireland

The Miscarriage Association of Ireland was founded in September 1988 by Hilary Frazer and is a registered charity. The Association is run by a committee of volunteers who themselves have experienced the loss of a baby through miscarriage.

The Miscarriage Association of Ireland provides peer-to-peer support, all the details of which can be found on our website miscarriage.ie.

The core supports we provide are;
· Telephone support (see website **miscarriage.ie** for numbers)
· Email support (info@miscarriage.ie)
· Group support meetings
· Annual Service of Remembrance
· Book of Remembrance
· Memorial Stones
· Information book
· Newsletter

In 1998 The Book of Remembrance was officially launched by Frances Fitzgerald TD in the College of Surgeons. This is an unofficial register for babies lost through miscarriage. It is a beautiful, leather-bound book and holds special memories of our precious little babies who only got the opportunity to share our lives for a short time. *"Their time was short, yet very precious"*.

To make an entry in the Book of Remembrance in memory of your baby - send an email with Book of Remembrance in the subject bar and your baby's name, dates, remembered by and any special thoughts (max five lines) and the entry will be made and a Remembrance Certificate sent to you via post.

THANK YOU

"Thank you to Dr. Siobhan Corcoran and the bereavement team at The National Maternity hospital, in particular Sarah Cullen. A special thank you to the mums who took the time to both write and share the stories of their little babies with us for this journal. It has been a privilege to both read and print them. They will never be forgotten. To Sarah Tobin who not only helped me but became my friend and together we were able to create this journal. To my husband for always being there and forever believing in me, Beau will always be part of us. Finally a huge thank you to my family and friends, especially Trish Gallagher who all supported and helped me on this." **Laura**

"Thank you to Dominique McMullen of IMAGE Magazine for editing the journal and to Sarah Hamill for the beautiful design. Thank you to Emma Flynn from This Mama Doodles for the beautiful illustration. Thank you to Lucinda Watkinson for reading an early version of this journal in the midst of her own grief, her feedback was so appreciated. Thank you to all my family and friends for their continued support since Alice was born, you have allowed her to have such a lasting legacy, of which Dave and I are so proud. And a final thank you to Laura for coming to me with this fantastic idea and a brilliant first draft of the journal, it's been such an honour to do this for all the babies in the sky." **Sarah**

A huge heartfelt thanks to all of the people who donated to this journal when it was just an idea. We appreciate the trust and faith they have given us both with their donations and support. The journal would not be here without you. Thank you too to the contributors to our survey, lots of which is included within the journal and will also feature online.

Thank you to Dan Mulcahy of Arrow Management for organising the printing of this journal.

We would both like to thank the charities mentioned for their enthusiasm and support in getting this journal distributed to the people who need it.

If you would like to share with us any feedback or suggestions for future versions, please contact us.

Laura & Sarah